About *Sophia Discovers the Real*

★★★★★ *"Must read...Sophia Discovers the Real Treasure* engenders a passion for the glorious wilderness and the indigenous people who once dwelled therein."

--Paulette Reefer, *Reedsy Discovery Reviews*

"If only one book about John Muir were to be selected for a discriminating picture book collection, it should be *Sophia Discovers the Real Treasure*."

--D. Donovan, Senior Reviewer, *Midwest Book Review*

"*Sophia Discovers the Real Treasure* will surely become a favorite with the young people in your life."

--Lisa Lickel, *Wisconsin Writers Association Book Review*

"It reads with the drama and excitement of fiction, but packs in much information about Native American and natural history as it reviews the political and social forces that influenced Muir's ability to save these lands for future generations."

--D. Donovan, Senior Reviewer, *Midwest Book Review*

"This wonderful picture book provides ideal reading for children as well as persons of all ages who enjoy reading."

--Paulette Reefer, *Reedsy Discovery Reviews*

Sophia Discovers the Real Treasure
A Story of John Muir, Father of the National Parks

By Curt Casetta

Edited by Christina Lloyd

ISBN: 978-1-956224-02-3

Published by Trenton House Publishing, West Bend, WI
TrentonHousePublishing.com
TrentonHousePublishing@gmail.com

Sophia
Discovers the Real Treasure

A Story of John Muir,
Father of the National Parks

by Curt Casetta

Foreword by Mike Wurtz

University of the Pacific

For harmony with the Earth

and harmony with one another

Author's note

Readers,

Please don't read just the story. It's important to read both the foreword and afterword sections, too. Then, just as importantly, discuss what you read with others.

The foreword, written by a John Muir scholar, shows John Muir's love for nature, especially for the sequoia trees he found in California.

The afterword discusses the horrible treatment towards Native Americans, especially in the California area, starting before John Muir arrived.

Each section shares valuable, extra details about John Muir and about the land that he, and the Native Americans, loved.

Foreword

John Muir and the Giant Sequoias are nearly synonymous. Shortly after arriving in California, Muir saw the groves, slept at their mammoth bases, and connected to the trees like the squirrels he saw leaping from their branches. "Greatest of trees, greatest of living things, their noble domes poised in unchanging repose seemed to belong to the sky."

 Always a botanist, Muir wanted to know everything he could about the most massive tree in the world. He spent months exploring sequoia groves, counting the rings of the downed trees, and trying to understand why they grew so big. He still wanted to be part of the trees themselves by drinking the sequoia cone tannin-laced water, hoping thereby to "improve my color and render myself more tree-wise and sequoical."

On those explorations, he came across mill sites that left groves of stumps and decided that the sequoias needed not only to be sought for light and studied, but to be protected. "Could one of these Sequoia Kings come to town in all its godlike majesty so as to be strikingly seen and allowed to plead its own cause, there would never again be any lack of defenders."

Muir's focus throughout his life was to preserve nature so generations to come can visit these places, rest, reconnect with the natural world…and hopefully talk with the sequoias. "Nature's peace will flow into you as sunshine flows into trees."

Mike Wurtz
Author of *John Muir's Grand Yosemite: Musings and Sketches*
Curator of John Muir Papers at the University of the Pacific

John Muir's Giant Sequoia

NPS Photo (JOMU)/Keith Park

John Muir loved the mountains and the enormous sequoia trees he found there. In 1885, John dug up a sequoia seedling and brought it home. He planted it on his wife's family fruit ranch, in a valley near Martinez, California (John moved his own family there five years later).

Sequoias can live thousands of years in the mountains. Different conditions in the valley, however, allowed the tree to become sick. The disease made it hard for the sequoia to get the water and nutrients it needed.

This sequoia that John Muir planted will die long before it would have died in the mountains. But the United States National Park Service found a way to grow copies of his tree, so another will be planted when that day comes.

In every walk with nature,
one receives far more than
he seeks.

-John Muir

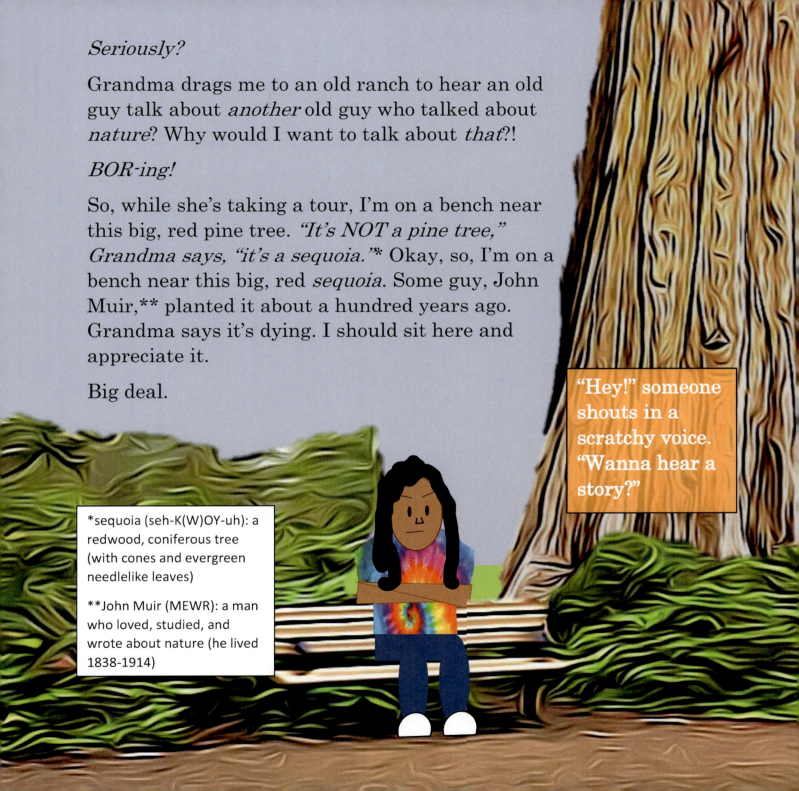

Seriously?

Grandma drags me to an old ranch to hear an old guy talk about *another* old guy who talked about *nature*? Why would I want to talk about *that*?!

BOR-ing!

So, while she's taking a tour, I'm on a bench near this big, red pine tree. *"It's NOT a pine tree," Grandma says, "it's a sequoia."** Okay, so, I'm on a bench near this big, red *sequoia*. Some guy, John Muir,** planted it about a hundred years ago. Grandma says it's dying. I should sit here and appreciate it.

Big deal.

"Hey!" someone shouts in a scratchy voice. "Wanna hear a story?"

*sequoia (seh-K(W)OY-uh): a redwood, coniferous tree (with cones and evergreen needlelike leaves)

**John Muir (MEWR): a man who loved, studied, and wrote about nature (he lived 1838-1914)

Now, *this* guy's interesting. He's got a gray, bushy beard, wild hair, a ragged, brown hat. And a *donkey*!

"You look like a prospector!" I shout. Prospectors looked for gold near here over 100 years ago. I read about them in school.

He nods with a wink. "You ain't no beef-headed greenhorn."

"Huh?" I say.

"Bored, are ya'?" he asks.

I shrug.

"Let me tell ya' about John Muir. Father of the National Parks."

"Hey! That's Grandma's *tree* guy!"

He nods. "I'm Big Red. But you can just call me Red."

Um, *brown* hat, *blue* jeans, *gray* hair. Okay. Sure. *Red*, it is.

Red smiles. "John never been bored. He appreciated the nature all around him."

He coughs. "You'll have to excuse me, I ain't been feeling too good."

He pats the donkey.

"Let's saunter, as John liked to call it. Maybe you'll find some treasure yourself."

"Treasure?!"

Red nods.

"*And* I get to ride the donkey?!"

Red shoots me a smile-less look.
"Mule," he says.

"Huh?"

"Jack's a mule. Not a donkey."

I hop on Jack, anyway.
"Let's go find some
treasure!!" I yell.

Red leads us down a trail. He limps. He wheezes. He doesn't seem to be doing too well, at all...

"Is this where the treasure is?" I ask.

Red smiles. "Don't worry. You'll find it."

Red starts his story. "John come from Scotland. He always loved nature. At age eleven, he moved to America. He called it a glorious wilderness."

0004080171Z

Strange, but it's evening now. I see trees, and tall grass, and flowers. No treasure, though.

"John even appreciated fireflies the first time he seen 'em," Red says. "There's him and his brother now."

Two kids are in the grass. They're laughing and running around. Little flashes of light are everywhere. I climb off Jack so I can run around, too.

"Such strange lights!"
cries one of the kids.

"They're fireflies," I
say. "Grandma calls
them lightning bugs."

We run. We laugh. It's fun. It's beautiful.

I never thought fireflies were fun *or*
beautiful before.

"Vamoose!" calls Red. "There's more to discover!"

I wanna stay, but I *really* wanna find that treasure.

"Should I get back on the donkey?" I ask.

Red shoots me his look.

"Mule," he says.

I nod and climb aboard. We travel between two hills. The sky's lighter now. Red's limp is getting worse. So's the wheezing.

"John appreciated nature," says Red.

I see a guy with a wild beard. He's drawing something.

"Here's John at age 29. He walked from Kentucky to Florida. About 1000 miles."

"A *thousand* miles?!" I gasp.

"Yup. And he drawed and wrote about the nature he seen."

I climb off Jack to take a look.

Maybe he's writing about the treasure!

Nope. There's drawings of trees. I read John's words:

The soft light of morning falls upon ripening forests of oak and elm, walnut and hickory and all Nature is thoughtful and calm.

I never noticed before. It *is* calm. And trees *do* look special in the morning sun.

"Let's go, whippersnapper."

Red means me. It's hard to leave this beautiful place.

I ask, "Back on the donk—?"

Red shoots me his look.

"I mean, back on the *mule*?" I say.

Red nods.

I climb up. We round the bend.

"After a bit," says Red, "John come to California."

Red stops to catch his breath.

"He come to a valley now called Yosemite,* before that, Ahwahnee.** The people who lived here called themselves Ahwahnechee.*** John appreciated this place. He said nature gathered its choicest treasures."

It *is* beautiful. There are majestic waterfalls. The river is rushing in the valley. I see trees and soaring, canyon walls. This is so beautiful, I don't care if we find any treasure or not.

*Yosemite (Yo-SEM-it-tee): thought to refer to certain Native American Miwuk (MEE-wuck) peoples who once lived in the valley.

**Ahwahnee (Ah-WAH-nee): in the Southern Sierra Miwuk language, thought to mean large mouth—what the cliff-lined valley looked like.

***Ahwahnechee (Ah-wah-NEE-chee): Native American people who once lived in Ahwahnee.

Red says, "John knew Yosemite better'n probably anybody."

"*Any*body?" I ask.

"Well," says Red, "the Native American Miwuk, Mono Lake Paiute, Chukchansi Yokuts, and Western Mono* peoples *did* care for this land for centuries."

He adds quietly, "But they was pretty much gone when John arrived."

"What do you mean, *gone*?"

"Well," says Red, "sometimes white folks moved in and took over because they wanted the land fer themselves—land that had provided acorns so important in the Native diet, hunting and fishing grounds, places that were sacred to Native Americans whose people had lived here for generations. Sometimes it was even done to clear the way for something like a National Park."

"But why?" I ask.

"The people moving in thought their ways was best."

"So, they asked the Native Americans to move?"

Red shakes his head. "Most of the time, white people forced 'em out. Sometimes the army made 'em go. Sometimes they even killed 'em."

"Oh, NO!," I cry.

Red's voice trembles. "That happened a lot back then."

*Miwuk (MEE-wuck), Mono Lake Paiute (MOH-noh Layk PY-oot), Chukchansi Yokuts (CHOOK-chan-see YO-kuts), Western Mono (MOH-noh): Native American peoples that once lived in or around the valley now known as Yosemite

After a few moments, I ask, "Did John ever meet any Native Americans?"

"He did," says Red.

"And they became friends?" I ask, hopefully.

Red sighs. "They lived different from John. They didn't look the same as him. At first, he described 'em as dirty and repellent."

"*Repellent*? Doesn't that mean *disgusting*?" I ask.

Red nods.

"That's horrible," I say.

"In John's time," says Red, "that's how some people talked about people who looked or lived different from them."

I can't believe what I'm hearing. "Why would they do that?"

"Well," Red says slowly, "some people are mean, pretending they're better'n others."

I feel like crying.

"And some," continues Red, "talked that way 'cause that's how the people around 'em talked."

I think about that. "Which kind of people was John?"

Red shakes his head. "I don't know."

"Neither of those sound right," I say.

I just stare at the ground. So does Red.

Red finally looks up. "Later, though, John got to know some Native Americans, and he come to respect them."

"He did?"

"Yup. He saw they appreciated nature, too. John learned Native Peoples weren't really so different from him, after all."

Red points to the valley. "John's real work was keeping Yosemite beautiful. He wrote about it so other folks would appreciate it, too."

"It *is* beautiful," I say.

"John stopped farmers from growing crops here. Stopped their animals from eatin' the greenery. Tried to keep folks from dammin' the rivers. Saved trees from getting cut down. John even brung a president campin' here to see its beauty."

"A President?"

Yup. President Teddy Roosevelt. And he appreciated it, too. Because of John, America started savin' more places like Yosemite for parks. That's why John's called the Father of the National Parks."

The trail gets steeper.

"Don't worry. I'm holding the…"

Red looks at me.

"…*mule*," I smile.

Red shoots me a grin.

"What about you?" I ask. "How did *you* meet John?"

Red scratches his beard. "Well, John loved saunterin' through nature."

"Like we did today…" I add.

Red coughs terribly.

"You okay?" I ask.

Red nods, then continues, "I come from the mountains. That's where John found me."

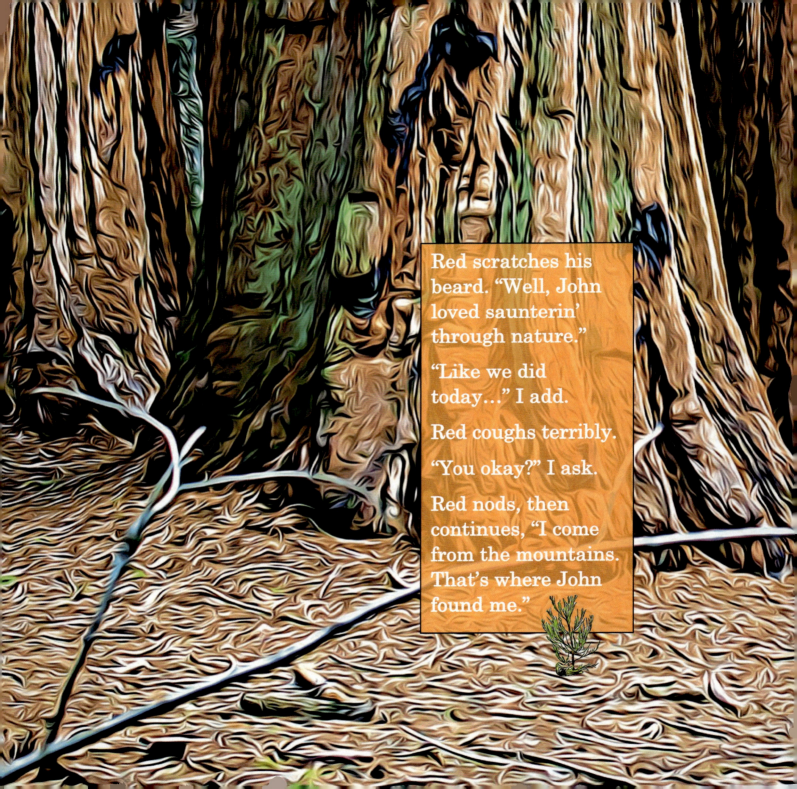

"I was a young 'un when John brung me here, where his wife's family run a fruit ranch."

I see the bench where we started.

"And John settled here to raise *his* family," says Red. "That included me."

"At *this* ranch…," I whisper.

Red nods. "But a ranch warn't no place for John. He needed to share the world's beauty. So, John sauntered."

"A-course I didn't go," says Red quietly. "I stayed here."

"But it's beautiful here, too," I offer.

Red looks towards the mountains. "Turns out a ranch ain't no place for me, neither."

"Huh?"

"John didn't know it," says Red between coughs, "and neither'd I. But being here made me sick."

"Oh, no."

Red sighs. "Just like John, my kind don't do so good unless we're in the mountains, too."

I hold back a tear.

"Did you know," Red asks, "that sequoia trees can live in the mountains for thousands of years?"

"You mean those big, red pines?"

Red chuckles. "Well, they ain't *pines*."

"I know…," I smile, "they're *sequoias*."

I climb off Jack. I sit on the bench where my wandering started.

"And when John left this Earth about a hundred years back, he figured I'd be here long after him."

"What do you mean?"

Red motions to the tree behind me.

I look up.

The needles are thinning. The red bark is fading. It's dying.

"I was a seedling when John brung me here. I reminded him of the mountains. He planted me in this spot about 140 years ago."

I appreciate it.

I really do.

I think about the National Parks John inspired people to save.

I remember how John sometimes described people that weren't like him.

I recall the Miwuk, forced from this beautiful land so long ago.

I give my friend, the big, red sequoia, a hug.

I head towards John's house.

I have some
things I want to
talk to
Grandma
about, after all.

Indigenous Peoples (Native Americans) lived in and took care of the Yosemite Valley long before the arrival of John Muir (1868), or that of white settlers or gold miners in 1848.

Afterword

John Muir came to Yosemite in 1868, after practically all Indigenous Peoples (Native Americans) had been erased from the landscape by white settlers. His earlier writings about Native Americans, although brief, were sometimes derogatory (similar to offensive attitudes toward non-white people held by many whites at the time), and he rarely addressed the horrible way they were treated.

Particularly with the Gold Rush in 1848, white settlers moved into California, eager to claim the land—and its riches—as their own. Government officials, wanting to rid the area of Indigenous people, gave white settlers rewards for killing Native Americans. The United States Army even helped with the slaughter. Thousands of

Native Americans were murdered. Others died from diseases introduced for which they had no immunity. Many were forced to flee. White settlers were even given the right to make Native children their slaves. Native cultures were disrupted or forever changed, with many virtually wiped out of existence.

The idea that "wilderness" had to be without people to preserve its beauty is a concept that was popular during Muir's time. Some dispute as to whether any land that had been inhabited and used by people could even be called a "wilderness," at all. Ultimately, however, this "wilderness" idea resulted in essentially all Indigenous people being removed from Yosemite, where their ancestors had lived for thousands of years.

John Muir, like most non-Native Americans, seemed not to appreciate the special knowledge and unique relationship that Indigenous people had, and still have, with the land in Yosemite.

The arrival of gold miners, beginning in 1848, brought disease, displacement, and death for many of California's Native Americans.

After Muir met Native Alaskans (the Tlingit) who had not suffered nearly to the extent of Native Californians, his respect for Indigenous Peoples grew, as reflected in his later writings and public comments. However, his earlier words and lack of understanding still cause pain for many people.

Even today, the effects of the removal of Indigenous Peoples are felt by their descendants. They have had to endure and overcome more than a century of stereotypes and discrimination. Some still seek recognition of their tribes and acknowledgement of their claims to the lands of their ancestors. They persevere in spite of such obstacles.

While people can celebrate the legacy that includes National Parks such as Yosemite, it must be mourned that it often came at the terrible expense of so many.

"That war of extermination will continue to be waged between the races until the Indian race becomes extinct must be expected."

—California Governor Peter Burnett, January 6, 1851

California's Governor predicted that California's Native Americans would be exterminated and become "extinct."

John Muir at about age 25

Timeline of John Muir's life

April 21, 1838	Born in Dunbar, Scotland
1849	Moves to Fountain Lake (Buffalo Township), Wisconsin, USA
1861	Attends college at the University of Wisconsin
1867	Begins his "Thousand-Mile Walk to the Gulf"
1868	Arrives by ship in San Francisco, walks to Yosemite
1879	First trip to Alaska to study glaciers, spends time there with Native American Tlingit (TLING-(g)it)
1880	Marries Louisa "Louie" Wanda Strentzel
1885	Replants sequoia seedling on his wife's family fruit ranch
1890	Moves (w/his wife and two daughters) to the fruit ranch
1890	Yosemite is declared a National Park
1892	Helps start the environmental organization, Sierra Club
1903	Camps with President Theodore Roosevelt at Yosemite
1906	The Mariposa Grove of Giant Sequoias becomes part of Yosemite National Park
December 24, 1914	Dies of pneumonia in Los Angeles, CA (age 76)

Image Courtesy of John Muir NHS, JOMU 4880_A1-34

John Muir's family home on the fruit ranch near Martinez, California (about 1900)

Image Courtesy of John Muir NHS (JOMU 4880_A1-34)

Image courtesy of John Muir NHS, JOMU 1732

John Muir with his family at their fruit ranch near Martinez, California, about 1902. From left, daughters Wanda and Helen, wife Louie, John (about age 64), and "Keeny" (one of many dogs he owned over the years named "Stickeen")

President Theodore "Teddy" Roosevelt visited Muir at Yosemite in 1903.

Everett Collection/Shutterstock.com

The sequoia called the "General Sherman Tree" is 275 feet tall and is the world's largest (by volume). It's in Sequoia National Park (southeast of Yosemite).

GENERAL SHERMAN

Muir played in and explored these fields as a boy next to his Fountain Lake (now Ennis Lake) home in Wisconsin.

The Miwuk used holes they created in nearby rock to grind seeds and acorns into meal. These grinding holes are still visible northwest of Yosemite.

Yosemite Falls actually has three parts: Upper Fall, the Middle Cascades, and Lower Fall. Altogether, it's more than 2400 feet high, one of the overall tallest waterfalls in the world. The main Ahwahnechee village was located near its base.

Muir studied glaciers here in what is now Alaska's Glacier Bay National Park. This glacier was named the "Muir Glacier" in his honor (it has gotten much smaller—receded—since Muir's first visit in 1879).

After white militia soldiers drove the Ahwahnechee from the Yosemite region, they named this lake "Tenaya Lake," to "honor" the Ahwahnechee's Chief Tenaya.* Tenaya is said to have told them, "It already has a name. We call it Py-we-ack."*

Muir built a cabin alongside Yosemite Creek and lived there from 1869-1871. It's the creek that later becomes Yosemite Falls.

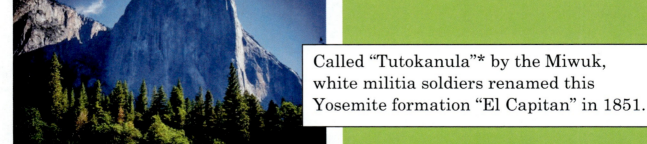

Called "Tutokanula"* by the Miwuk, white militia soldiers renamed this Yosemite formation "El Capitan" in 1851.

*Please note that spellings may vary

Bibliography

Blakemore, Erin, *California's Little-Known Genocide* (November 16, 2017, updated December 4, 2020), retrieved from www.history.com/news/californias-little-known-genocide, March, 2021.

Brune, Michael, *Pulling Down Our* Monuments, (July 22, 2020), retrieved from www.sierraclub.org/michael-brune/2020/07/john-muir-early-history-sierra-club, August, 2020.

Bunnell, Lafayette H., *Discovery of the Yosemite* (1892), retrieved from www.yosemite.ca.us/library/discovery_of_the_yosemite/, February, 2021.

Burnett, California Governor Peter, State of the State Address, January 6, 1851, retrieved from https://governors.library.ca.gov/addresses/s_01-burnett2.html, January, 2022.

Clark, Galen, *Indians of the Yoesmite and Vicinity* (1904), retrieved from www.yosemite.ca.us/ library/indians_of_the_yosemite/, February, 2021.

Clarke, Chris, *Untold History: The Survival of California Indians* (September 26, 2016), retrieved from www.kcet.org/shows/tending-the-wild/untold-history-the-survival-of-californias-indians, March 2021.

Farquhar, Francis P., *Place Names of the High Sierra* (1926), retrieved from www.yosemite.ca.us/library/place_names_of_the_high_sierra/c.html, February, 2022.

Gold, Greed, and Genocide, International Indian Treaty Council, www.iitc.org/gold-greed-genocide/, retrieved March, 2021.

Highland, Chris, *Ancoutahan: John Muir Among the Native Peoples*, (2014, updated 2018), www.sierraclub.org/john_muir_exhibit/life/ancoutahan-john-muir-among-native-peoples.aspx, retrieved September, 2020.

John Muir, National Park Service, retrieved from www.nps.gov/yose/learn/historyculture/muir.htm, June, 2019.

John Muir's Giant Sequoia, Atlas Obscura, www.atlasobscura.com/places/john-muirs-giant-sequoia, retrieved June, 2019.

Muir, John, *A Thousand Mile Walk to the Gulf* (1916), retrieved from www.yosemite.ca.us/john_muir_writings/a_thousand_mile_walk_to_the_gulf/, August, 2019.

Muir, John, *My First Summer in the Sierra* (1911), retrieved from www.yosemite.ca.us/john_muir_writings/my_first_summer_in_the_sierra/my_first_summer_in_the_sierra.pdf, August, 2019.

Southern Sierra Miwuk Nation Narrative, retrieved from www.southernsierramiwuknation.org/federal-recognition, February, 2021.

Spence, Mark, *Dispossessing the Wilderness: Yosemite Indians and the National Park Ideal, 1864-1930*, Pacific Historical Review, Vol. 65, No. 1 (Feb., 1996), University of California Press, retrieved from http://www.jstor.org/stable/3640826, February, 2021.

The Southern Sierra Miwuk Nation: Yosemite Mariposa's First People, Yosemite Mariposa County Tourism Board, retrieved from www.yosemite.com/yosemite-mariposas-first-people/, January, 2022.

Traditionally Associated Tribes of Yosemite National Park, *Voices of the People* (Yosemite Conservancy, 2021).

Yosemite Firefall, retrieved from https://yosemitefirefall.com/yosemite-firefall-horsetail-fall, February, 2022.

Acknowledgments

P.7, Muir's Giant Sequoia, NPS Photo (JOMU)/ Keith Park

P.20, Muir Portrait, MSS 48 F23-1246, John Muir Papers, Holt-Atherton Special Collections, University of the Pacific Library © 1984 Muir-Hanna Trust (head)

P.22, Muir Writing, John Muir Journals, *July 1867-February 1868, the "thousand-mile walk" from Kentucky to Florida*

P. 40, Hills Surrounding Muir Home Site, NPS Photo (JOMU)/Keith Park (digitally-altered)

P.42, Muir House, NPS Photo (JOMU)/Luther Bailey (digitally-altered)

P. 45, California Governor Peter Burnett quote, *State of the State Address*, January 6, 1851.

P.46, John Muir Portrait (circa 1863), MSS 48 F23-1247, John Muir Papers, Holt-Atherton Special Collections, University of the Pacific Library © 1984 Muir-Hanna Trust

P.47, Muir House, courtesy of John Muir NHS (JOMU 4880_A1-34)

P.62, Muir Family, courtesy of John Muir NHS (JOMU 1732)

Additional photos: Viktoriia Bondar (p.6); Mike Wurtz (p.6); Morphart Creations (p.8); Maarten Brand (p.43); Everett Collection (p.44); Everett Collection/Shutterstock.com (p.49a); Logga Wiggler (p.49b); Curt Casetta (p.49c); Iulian Ursache (p.50a); Jeffrey Banke (p.50b); Steve Prorak (p.50c); Peter Perhac (p.51a); Goldilock Project (p. 51b); André Cook (p.3,51c); Andrew S (p.55); BeFunky; Shutterstock

Special thanks to

Mike Wurtz (Assistant Professor/Head of Holt-Atherton Special Collections and Archives, University of the Pacific)

Liz Williams, Tribal Liaison, Yellowstone National Park

Virginia Bones (Museum Curator, John Muir National Historic Site)

Keith Park, National Park Service

Luther Bailey, National Park Service

Leah Jurss, Jacob Jurss, Jodi Casetta, Gabrieellea Kidd

Many voices that prefer to remain unnamed

Other books by Curt Casetta

Sophia Saves the Earth

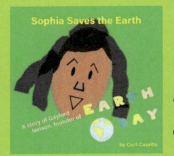

A Story of Gaylord Nelson, Founder of Earth Day

"...an inspiration to children everywhere," daughter of Gaylord Nelson, climate activist Tia Nelson

"...exciting and immediate to young readers...a great gift to any child and also the future of the Earth," Nancy Lorraine, *Midwest Book Review*

The Kids of Willow Lane: Fun Poems by Curt Casetta

"An adorable and entertaining book!" Children's author Brenda E. Cortez, *Howl the Owl* books

Bluebell Saves the Day (Bluebell Saves the Day Adventure #1)

Bluebell and the Runaway Bus (Bluebell Saves the Day Adventure #2)

Bluebell and the Fancy-Schmancy Car (Bluebell Saves the Day Adventure #3)

Bluebell's Perfect Christmas (Bluebell Holiday Adventure #1)

Connect with Curt at CasettaKids.com

Made in the USA
Las Vegas, NV
23 February 2022

44413517R20036